PowerProject
INSTITUTE

The Power of Engagement

Includes the Innovation & Engagement at Work Scale™

Copyright © 2013 Pamela J Green
All rights reserved.
ISBN: 0988680416
ISBN 13: 9780988680418
Library of Congress Control Number: 2013930165
Power Project Institute, LLC

Table of Contents

A. Key Drivers of Engagement 1

B. Innovation and Engagement at Work 5

C. Effective Listening 11

D. Leadership Is Action—Not Position 15

E. Using the Instrument 19

F. Characteristics 27

G. Assessing the Stress Effect 33

H. How Do You Know for Certain? 39

I. Addressing Performance 47

J. Change Management 55

K. Why Typical Engagement Strategies Won't Work for Everyone 61

L. The Engagement Process 69

M. Bottom Line: Hand Them the Keys 75

N. Measuring Success 81

O. Bibliography 87

P. About PPI 89

Key Drivers of Engagement

"I'm not concerned with your liking or disliking me...all I ask is that you respect me as a human being."

— Jackie Robinson

Engagement is what happens when a person feels respected. There are many ways to demonstrate respect, but in the work environment performers want to be respected for their ideas, their experiences, their contributions, and their results. When you respect what a performer brings to the table, and who he or she is, productivity will increase. The challenge many leaders face is in how to demonstrate that respect. With respect comes action, and it is that action that leads to engagement. If a leader merely says, "Wow, that is a great idea," and does nothing further, then the employee feels good in the moment, but that feeling diminishes quickly when the leader does not act on the "great idea." When a leader shows respect to a performer, the following results may appear:

- The employees are given opportunities to get involved in decision-making activities.
- The employees feel able to voice their ideas.
- The employees feel the manager is listening to them.
- The employees are encouraged and given opportunities to develop professionally.
- The employees are recognized for good work.
- The employees feel the company is concerned for their health and welfare.

If, at the very basic level, a leader is not demonstrating respect for a performer, regardless of whether the leader likes the performer (we will discuss this further), the engagement level will be low, and thus productivity will diminish. The premise of this book is to help people managers with the very basic element of employee engagement—showing respect. Using the guide below, you can see the varying degrees of influence and control you can have on an employee's experience:

Within The Employee's Complete Control	
Personality	**Performance**
Is the employee someone people want to work with?	Does the employee's performance consistently exceed expectations?

Within The Company's Complete Control		
People	**Policies**	**Politics**
Are the right people in the right place?	Are the written rules aligned with the company growth strategy?	Are the unspoken and unwritten rules of engagement helping or hindering productivity?

Joint Decisions for the Employee and Supervisor	
Progress	**Pulling-Out**
If 1-5 is in place, is the employee stepping up to the plate and giving their best performance? If yes, in what ways are they being rewarded and recognized?	Is it time for the employee to move on either because they've gone as far as they can or they find that this isn't a good fit for them after all? Review the I&E Scale first.

Many companies can save money on expensive, outside-engagement programs by simply listening to what the employees are telling them; showing respect for the people they have responsibility over; and leading effectively in the areas of people, politics, and policies over which the companies have direct influence and control. Use this guide as a reminder of what you already know: take care of the employee, and the employee will take care of you.

Innovation and
Engagement at Work

Despite all our gains in technology, product innovation and world markets, most people are not thriving in the organizations they work for.

— Stephen Covey

Innovation and Engagement at Work Scale™

High	The Trapped Worker	The Entrepreneur
Turnover	Satisfied Performers	
	The Checked Out	The Up and Comer
Low	Low **Innovation** High	

Today, many organizations are opting for changes in their working paradigm, and this can occur because of a variety of reasons, such as the devaluation of the brand, younger competition, or outdated machinery and management techniques. More often than not, an organization initiates change because of either growing demand or falling profits. Regardless of the reason the change is needed, it is vitally important that your people resources are on board with the change and are equipped and ready to support and see the change through. A company that does a poor job of engaging its workers will find that making needed changes in their working paradigm will be difficult.

Employee engagement is reported to be one of the most important factors for corporate success now and will be into the immediate future for any company looking to sustain itself over the long haul. In recent reports, Gallup estimates that the cost of disengagement in the United States is at a staggering $300 billion in lost productivity annually. Threats of an impending global talent war have many corporate leaders worried about whether they will have the talent needed to drive corporate profits. Already, while we are seeing that in many parts of the world available talent stands ready to be employed, company's are concerned that available talent is lacking the skills necessary to quickly close the talent gap that exists. Some argue that it is better for a company to train an under- or over-skilled candidate rather than leave a key position open. Others say that perhaps a company's first step is to look internally for ways to engage overlooked and underutilized talent. Still others say the answer lies in leadership. In fact, all three points are valid and there exists plenty of talent with transferrable skills just outside the corporate doors; however, internally, few leaders have the time, or maybe even the expertise, to truly analyze exactly which skills are transferrable to a particular job.

In our own research, Power Project Institute, LLC found that, of the more than five hundred people surveyed and 228 business leaders interviewed, 68 percent of those surveyed indicated the biggest challenges going into 2013 include the following issues:

1. Low morale because of poor economy or other factors;
2. Lack of good pay, benefits, and paid time off;
3. No upward mobility or opportunities for promotion.

A staggering 72.8 percent of those surveyed didn't know what low employee engagement was costing their company! Of the 64 percent who are participating in some type of engagement activities, 90 percent say the engagement activities are being provided by internal resources, yet most reported being unhappy with those internal initiatives.

So then, what is a leader to do who needs to attract and retain critical talent? The answer may start by building a reputation for engagement. Being the boss may sound like a good thing, but is more often a headache when you actually reach the top. This difficulty is because, like the employees you have responsibility for, leaders face a unique set of challenges that comes part-and-parcel from being where all the decisions are made. The key to a successful business is good leadership and having a style of leadership that enhances company performance.

A self-help guru once defined leadership as simply the ability to make things happen using the help of other people's skills and abilities. Some leaders are quite gifted from birth, but many other leaders must go through leadership development to hone those leadership skills properly.

If engagement is truly to work, it will require much more of the leader than of the employees initially. Leaders themselves must evaluate their leadership style and be willing to make adjustments to meet the employees' and the company's needs. There is a style of leadership behavior that might work well in one company but does not bode well in another. Leaders who fail to recognize this not only jeopardize the reputation, growth, and success of the company, but also the productivity of the employees for whom they are in charge.

Besides employees who lack engagement, it is entirely possible that the needs of the workforce are surpassing the capabilities of its present leaders. Meaning, the way most corporations are run today are akin to the leadership mindset of the laws, rules, and regulations that came into play in the 1950s and 60s, and some might argue even earlier than that. Political rules from more than fifty years ago lie beneath the thin veneer of physical rules and regulations that govern many organizations and drive the engagement of today's employees. These include the following political rules:

- Pay your dues.
- Dress the part you want, not the part you have.
- Our opinion is your opinion.
- Tow the company line.

- Demonstrate commitment.
- I need to see you to know you are working.

These are all very familiar sayings that, to many professionals, simply are not applicable in today's world of work, but are still very prevalent in the thoughts of leaders.

> *Companies often focus on retaining star performers or leadership talent, overlooking pivotal roles—jobs that have an outsized ability to create (or destroy) the value customers expect.*
>
> PricewaterhouseCoopers
>
> <u>*10 Minutes on Engaging Your Pivotal Talent*</u>

So then, how does a leader who has been taught or trained in this way of thinking break free in such a way that it doesn't destroy the fabric of the company—although it may rip a little? The answer is easy, but the ensuing behavior is not: shift the focus to the employee, thus the birth of employee engagement. Regardless of whether you are considered a powerful, perfectionist, peaceful, or popular leader, you can make the shifts necessary to engage employees in meaningful ways.

Effective Listening

*One of the most sincere forms of respect is
actually listening to what another has to say.*

— *Bryant H. McGilld*

Effective Listening

Being an effective leader is tied to being an effective listener.

All too often we are far more enthusiastic about talking than we are about listening. Yet listening is so vital if we are to communicate effectively. Most breakdowns in leadership effectiveness are a result of the two-way monologue: people talking at each other without really making contact. Unless someone hears what has been said, including the subtext, the words have little value.

When employees are actively listened to, they feel valued and are far more likely to engage in meaningful conversation and compromise, which results in greater productivity. Remember, you may be trying to get them to move from a tightly-held position of status quo, or to get them to move in an entirely different and uncomfortable direction altogether. Therefore, you'll have to relax your stance, listen to and address their objections, concerns, fear, and conjecture. You may not land on a place of agreement with the answers you provide them; however, you can put them at ease if they believe that no matter what happens, you are in this together. Heading into a difficult season of growth, or change in strategic direction, will be much easier if your employees trust you as their leader.

Trust begins with being a good listener, and listening is about far more than words. Watching facial expressions and body language is often a far more accurate barometer than the words being used. To be an effective listener, it is vital that you listen actively.

Ten tips to becoming a more effective listener are listed below:

1. Make eye contact.
2. Read the employee's body language. Is the employee relaxed, anxious, or angry? Extremes are easy to recognize, but often the message is much more subtle.

3. Subtly mirror the employee's body language—a gentle dance rather than a caricature.

4. Show that you are listening. Nod and make appropriate, genuine responses.

5. Ask relevant questions. Ask the employee to clarify if you are not clear about their meaning.

6. Summarize: "So what I hear you saying is..."

7. Use open-ended questions—the who, what, where, when—to make the employee feel their ideas, thoughts, and suggestions are worth listening to.

8. Be careful of the tone of your voice when you respond or ask questions. It is all too easy to come across as judgmental or as an interrogator, especially for those with intimidating leadership styles.

9. Use empathy. Acknowledge difficulties, but be careful not to fall into the trap of going into anecdotes from your experience. "I sense that you are finding this rather difficult," rather than "Oh, I know, it happened to me, but mine was bigger, more difficult, etc."

10. Take a real interest. If you are simply going through the motions, the lack of sincerity will be obvious to others. Leave your ego behind and concentrate on the message the employee is trying to convey.

Most employees will flourish in a work environment with clear direction, encouragement, and support. Without at least these three things, employees are sometimes easily and quickly cast aside, or they merely self-select out of the company.

Leadership Is Action —
Not Position

A good leader is one who can tell another how to reach his or her potential; a great leader is one who can help another discover this potential for him or herself.

— Bo Bennett

Leadership Is Action—Not Position

People respond to good leadership! Period! This is true in all aspects of our lives, not just business. A mother is a leader on her job; a son may be leader of a team sport, or a daughter the leader of the debate team. A group relies on the person in charge to actually lead them to success. A true leader is highly ethical, honest, respected as a person and for their position, and seems to have all of these attributes in place:

- Leaders think *big!* They do not put a ceiling in place. Instead, no limit is set for how big or how much better something can be.

- The goals are firmly set in place and the leader never loses sight of them.

- Leaders make known, to all involved, the final outcome for which they are all aiming. For example, if you sell widgets, you know that it will take X number of widgets to achieve a financial goal and other targets. Leaders know what the goal is and they ensure the team is also on board.

- Leaders can get compliance to orders without invoking fear or intimidation.

- Leaders set new goals or raise the bar when previous goals are met.

People will follow your lead willingly if you are honest, ethical, consistent, and treat them with respect. Rewarding someone when a job is well done is always appreciated. A good leader will also help an inconsistent performer move on—whether the performer is one who hinders the group, or one who has just decided not to be a team player.

Using the Instrument

Using The Instrument

Instead of casting off an apparent disengaged employee, the goal of the I&E Work Scale, can help leaders identify employees who appear most at risk, and it offers suggestions on ways to begin to engage employees who might fall into one of these main categories. Ultimately, the goal is to make employees more resourceful and accountable for achieving their goals and make the company more profitable or successful.

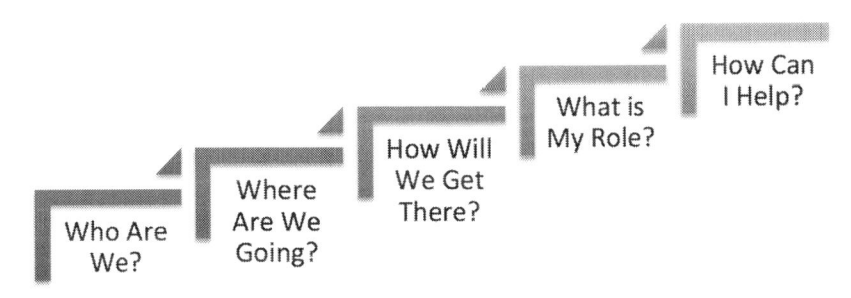

Who Are We? → Where Are We Going? → How Will We Get There? → What is My Role? → How Can I Help?

Before we get into the characteristics of employee engagement, a supervisor reviewing this instrument needs to ensure that the employee can affirm that the supervisor has addressed the following before they have a coaching conversation:

- Check 1: (Who are we?) Many believe. "Companies are ideas." In order for an idea to take on some form of growth and progression, someone else has to buy into it! Leaders must ensure that their talent—all of their talent—understands the company, and not just what they see in commercials, print, or social media. The employees should not know their company by what they find in The Glass Door or The Vault, websites that offer individuals the inside scoop on a particular company as reported by its current and former talent. They need to hear directly from their leader, and then other company leaders, exactly who the company is and what it is about in a consistent message. Not only do they need to know what the company stands for, but, in order to buy-into that idea, they must see it lived out in their presence. Their first standard of judgment is in how they believe they are valued.

- Check 2: (Where are we going?) The supervisor affirms that the employee knows where the company is headed—its goals, how it makes money, and where they are most at financial risk. If an employee can't articulate this information, this becomes step one: making sure employees know where the company is headed. If we are sitting in a boat together, we won't get to where we are going unless we row in the same direction. Does the employee sitting in your office, with an oar in hand, know which direction you are headed? Is he or she supportive or secretly sabotaging the mission?

- Check 3: (How are we going to get there?) The supervisor affirms employees know the methods the company plans to use to achieve its stated goals for the year. Do they know if the company plans to grow by hiring new talent, adding equipment, increasing sales goals, or adding services on the horizon? What information about the methods for growth would be useful for employees to be able to buy into the direction the company is headed?

- Check 4: (What is my role?) This is about role clarity and responsibility. For optimal engagement, employees have a need to know how they can help the company achieve its goals. This is the opportunity for you to uncover those with hidden potential and to engage those early-potential performers who have been waiting to share their transforming idea or demonstrate a particular skill or talent. This step really goes beyond their role and into their person. This is where you make the conversation personal and speak to who they are—their experiences, credentials, ideas, thoughts, and skills, etc. This conversation becomes the dragnet for everything they have ever learned or experienced, and how they can apply it to the job to make themselves and the company more successful. Instead of saying, "As an Uber Pooper Scooper, how does your job with the Pooper Scooper Company help us achieve our goals?" Their obvious answer will be, "Well, by scooping poop, I am helping the company be successful." Now what? Try instead, "John, based on your collective experiences, time on the job, education, and skills, when you think about what you do here, is there anything we have missed or overlooked in how the work is designed? Have you thought of any better, unique, or different ways of doing what you do?" If after an engaging conversation with the employee, he or she doesn't seem to know how to help, give the employee some ideas, or hints about how he or she can help the company achieve its goals. If this is your first time having such a conversation, an employee may not want to put himself or herself "out there" until he or she is comfortable with this line of questioning. This is a signal that there may be trust issues. To reinforce employees' suggestions, give them room to try an idea or two—without the fear of failure—by letting them know the risks associated with what they are attempting, and then show support even if it doesn't work.

- Check 5: (How can I help?) This final check is the most important and can solidify the acceptance by the employee. "John, as you know our goal at the company is to ensure all pet-friendly communities are free of unwanted pet debris and that the debris is properly recycled. However, we have only one percent of HOA communities signed on, and our goal is to grow to three percent this year. What are your thoughts about how we can achieve this goal this year? As we look at doing new or different things, is there a particular area of interest you have in helping us achieve our goals?" This will absolutely take him beyond his role and his thinking about the company. This is okay, because your job as a leader is to coach him into a discussion that is productive and actionable. This goes beyond his role and moves him from silo thinking to corporate thinking. Make note, however, of his earth-shattering thoughts as they may lead you to your next financial breakthrough. Most leaders reading this will say, "Yeah, and now I have to reel him back in." Maybe, but make employees responsible for reporting back any findings they have when they start connecting with others in the company. Then you can properly coach and direct them.

"The largest percentage of HR professionals surveyed indicated that their organizations were very likely to engage in transparent communication with employees regarding the status of the organization."

The Post Recession Workplace
Competitive Strategies for Recovery and Beyond
Research by the Society for Human Resource Management

Keep in mind that people can, and often do, move from one category of the I&E Scale to the next depending on their level of engagement in the organization. As you read each category, you might think back on your own performance experiences and how you were encouraged to move the needle. The ultimate goal is to get everyone to the Satisfied Performer status, because therein is balance. The Satisfied Performer is one who can get results, is recognized, and feels respected as a consistent performer. Why would I want my Entrepreneur and my Up-and-comer employees to move to the Satisfied Performer status? Isn't that movement just status quo? All four surrounding categories are extremes. The goal is to move people to a place where they are consistently productive, some more than others, but at least at a predictable rate.

Highly innovative and entrepreneurial performers can sometimes be so performance- and achievement-oriented that they ignore how important it is to work through systems, cultures, and people. Transversely, those with lower innovation and less of an entrepreneurial spirit may lack the social or communication skills, or the expertise, for getting their ideas communicated. Without guidance or assistance, these individuals may fall behind or run into career/performance snags. Once you determine what CAB (conduct, attitude, and behavior) they are driving, you can help them get to the right place safe and on time. Let's examine these more closely:

- Conduct is how a person carries himself or herself professionally and personally. Conduct is a person's demeanor and typical way of conducting himself or herself.

- Attitude is characteristic of what a person says and the non-verbal cues through body language. Attitude may also be reflected in the tone by which a message is conveyed and therefore is what determines the atmosphere that is created around the person.

- Behavior relates to the observable physical performance of an employee. Behavior also determines the degree of productivity and output by a performer.

Based on these three things, you should have a good sense of which category of innovation and engagement a particular employee falls within by reading the descriptions below.

Characteristics

In business, words are words; explanations are explanations, promises are promises, but only performance is reality.

— Harold S. Geneen

Characteristics

Trapped Workers (High Turnover/Low Innovation)

This worker has a lot to give, but feels stuck, and has a tendency to run into internal walls. Long-term marginalized people fall into this bucket. This category is typically characteristic of those with six to ten-plus years in one company. They are feeling that there is nothing better out there, so they just stay and play it safe, turning into below-the-radar employees, even though they have the potential to offer more. Some can get so comfortable that they have the tendency to become internal bullies to protect their turf and political position in company. They can feel easily threatened by newcomers. While length of service and minimal growth is a major factor, leaders should be especially careful not to ignore those performers with hidden potential and early-potential performers, who without development and proper engagement could develop this mentality. The moment they get a chance to break free, they are gone!

- They ask: Who is at fault?
- They respond: It wasn't me, not my fault!
- They think: Where will I go? Who would hire me?
- They feel: Trapped

Entrepreneurs (High Turnover/High Innovation)

These performers are often hired because of their enthusiasm, track record, penchant for great ideas, and because they epitomize what every company wants: energy, innovation, motivation, and enthusiasm. Unfortunately, these bright shining stars are often met with a culture that, in their opinion, may be viewed as counterproductive, slow paced, and bogged down by company politics. They are hired for their potential to offer a fresh perspective; however, they often leave or are fired after short periods of time because they are not properly assimilated or engaged. They do not necessarily want to move up in the organization. Many times they just want their voices heard and to be recognized for their contributions. Many times you will hear the words, "bad fit" when things do not work out for these performers. Leaders need to work with HR on proper assimilation strategies and coaching to ensure a successful fit for the organization.

- They ask: What can we do that is unique, different, or better?
- They respond: Yes, I'm willing to try it.
- They think: We keep doing the same things, expecting different results.
- They feel: Undervalued and underutilized

Satisfied Performers

These individuals are satisfied workers. They have achieved the level of success that works for them—for now. They are not trying to climb any ladders or compete for a job or status in the company. They simply want to perform a good job and continue to work. Their ambition is to continue to do a good job and be recognized for it. Leaders, be aware of how these performers want to be recognized. Some will be satisfied with the current pay system, others may want more money year after year, there may be those who want a title change, and those who may simply want to remain autonomous in their job. If the environment is good, as a leader, ask yourself, "How do I keep it this way?" Otherwise, you risk moving this performer to one of the other four quadrants.

- They ask: How can I help?
- They respond: I would be happy to help.
- They think: I am satisfied doing what I do.
- They feel: Respected, Recognized, and Engaged

Checked Out Performers (Low Turnover/Low Innovation)

These performers are not interested in learning any more than absolutely necessary. Often they make it known how many more years, months, weeks, or days they have to retire, followed up by status quo behavior of coasting or doing just enough to get by. Newer entrants into the group may simply be waiting out a leadership change and so adopt behaviors that keep them at status quo until either a new leader is named or they are forced to change. New ideas and innovative concepts are often met with great resistance from these employees, or supervisors, who may appear to lack the energy and enthusiasm to implement something new. Transversely, they may appear on board with an idea, but use passive-aggressive behaviors to avoid moving the project forward. This may be because they do not want to feel obligated to see it through to completion; they don't see the need to do things differently, especially if the current system doesn't appear broken; or perhaps it would require them to learn a challenging new skill set. Leaders should keep in mind that these people do not necessarily display bad attitudes, but keep an eye out for those who give good lip service with poor follow-through.

- They ask: Is this critical?
- They respond: Sure, it's possible.
- They think: It may be possible, but not probable.
- They feel: Unmotivated

Up-and-Comers (Low Turnover/High Innovation)

These individuals are often identified as high-potential employees—having great ideas and offering fresh perspectives—but because they might lack visibility, experiential credibility, or some other key skill set or capability, can find their growth stunted because of the heavy burden of corporate politics. Turnover is high, but it is lower than the Entrepreneurial Spirit of these innovative and energetic employees. They will usually quit after some time of trying to move up, but failing because of the lack of exposure, opportunity, marginalization, and the lack of senior leaders willing to sponsor them. Their goal is to find a job or career path that tests their limits. Leaders need to consider the politics of engagement and moving up in the organization, and work to create support systems for these performers. They will stay long enough to test the system, but not much longer.

- They ask: How can I help? Can I join a particular project? Have you thought about xyz?
- They respond: I'm willing to help.
- They think: This company is slow paced and not progressive.
- They feel: Frustrated and disenfranchised.

It is important to note that the further to the left the performer, the more difficult it will be to motivate and move them up, further on, or out of the company. Those performers to the right of the scale tend to remove themselves from less-productive and less-supportive work environments sooner rather than later. Below are some ways to assess if you have a particular performer who is at risk in one of the categories.

Assessing the
Stress Effect

Its not stress that kills us, it is our reaction to it.

— *Hans Selye*

Assessing the Stress Effect

The World Health Organization (WHO) conducted some research on the effects of stress on the workforce. This is an important factor because we wonder what pushes people from one category to the next and there could be a direct link to their ability or inability to manage stress properly. According to WHO, the following are some of the stress-related hazards challenging performers:

Job content:

- monotonous, under-stimulating, meaningless tasks
- lacking variety
- unpleasant tasks
- aversive tasks

Workload and work pace:

- having too much or too little to do
- working under time pressures

Working hours:

- strict and inflexible working schedules
- long and unsocial hours
- unpredictable working hours
- badly designed shift systems

Participation and control issues:

- lack of participation in decision making
- lack of control (for example, over work methods, work pace, working hours, and the work environment)

Work context concerns:

- career development, status, and pay
- job insecurity
- lack of promotion prospects
- under-promotion or over-promotion
- work of "low social value"
- piece-rate payments schemes
- unclear or unfair performance evaluation systems
- being over-skilled or under-skilled for the job

Role in the organization issues:

- an unclear role
- conflicting roles within the same job
- responsibility for people
- continuously dealing with other people and their problems

Interpersonal relationship hazards:

- inadequate, inconsiderate, or unsupportive supervision
- poor relationships with coworkers
- bullying, harassment, and violence
- isolated or solitary work
- no agreed procedures for dealing with problems or complaints

Organizational culture:

- poor communication
- poor leadership
- lack of clarity about organizational objectives and structure

Home-to-work interface concerns:

- conflicting demands of work and home
- lack of support at work for domestic problems at home
- lack of support at home for problems at work

Source: World Health Organization. Protecting Workers' Health Series No 3. Work Organization & Stress. "Systematic Problem Approaches for Employers, Managers, and Trade Union Representatives."

Sometimes it is difficult for us, as leaders, to realize the impact the workload, the environment, or even the hidden influences, have on an individual performer. Before you can explore further or jump to conclusions, we must ask ourselves, how much of the information above is posing a risk to the individual, to the team, to the completion of the assignment or work, or to the company? Ensuring that the company has a system of resources available to employees for handling or managing stress is vitally important to the mental and emotional health and safety of the individual and the company. A company must also ensure its supervisors are trained to recognize changes in behavior, mood, and attitude as not the employee's problem but as the organization's problem. A healthy worker makes for a healthy operation.

How Do You Know for Certain?

Knowledge speaks, but wisdom listens.

—Jimi Hendrix

How Do You Know for Certain

The Trapped Worker

- Are they inexperienced for the job they now hold?
- Do they miss deadlines or other important targets or goals?
- Do they lack key skills or qualifications?
- Is there a credibility issue due to a flaw in their conduct, attitude and/or behavior?
- Are they unable to maneuver the corporate political environment?
- Do they lack political savvy?
- Do they lack sensitivity to others?
- Does there appear to be a disconnect between what is/is not appropriate?
- Do they lack the ability to be confidential?
- Are they a poor read of people?
- Are they too candid?
- Do the exhibit poor interpersonal skills?

The Entrepreneur

- Do they get excited about doing new things or testing new concepts?
- Do they contribute a fare share of new or innovative ideas or suggestions for improvements?
- Do their ideas seem so innovative that they may appear a little off base?
- Are they self-motivated?
- Are they always looking to learn more?
- Are they broadly experienced?
- Do they make political missteps?
- Are they widely viewed as overly ambitious?
- Can generate new ideas but unable to create related strategies?
- Unable to swing from strategic to tactical and vise versa when called to do so.

The Satisfied Performer

- Can be counted on to deliver consistent results.
- Is a respected performer
- Good understanding of the direction of the business
- Are customer focused.
- Is a respected performer
- Good understanding of business direction
- Know how to find solutions to challenges.
- Career goals align with business direction.
- Seen as a team player.
- The employee is likeable.
- Content in current role, but could be considered for a more visible or promotional opportunity if good fit.
- Appears well balanced personally and professionally.
- Accept challenge in current role
- Is often used to help onboard new hires.
- Though not perfect does possess admirable conduct, attitude and behavior.

The Checked Out

- Do they consistently resist change initiatives?
- Do they demonstrate passive aggressive behaviors?
- Do they resist learning something new as it relates to their particular job?
- Are they comfortable operating in the status quo? (So it may appear they are a Satisfied Performer)
- Is their performance marginal at best?
- Do they rely too heavily on one set of skills or strengths for performance?
- Assess their level of engagement as it relates to contributing new ideas.
- Do they have difficulty with follow-through?
- Do they consistently miss deadlines?
- Are they, in general, disengaged, seem as if their mind is elsewhere?

The Up and Comer

- Do they lack humility?
- Do they relish being the center of attention?
- Are they unable or unwilling to admit mistakes?
- Are they unclear on how to align their career with company goals?
- Not a good listener?
- Do they appear overly competitive?
- Unable to have successful collaborative work relationships?
- Difficulty grasping strategic perspectives?
- Do they lack key skills or qualifications?
- Are they unable to maneuver the corporate political environment?
- Does there appear to be a disconnect between what is/is not appropriate?
- Are they a poor read of people?
- Are they not seen as resourceful?
- Do they rely too much on one particular strength?

If you are still unsure which category a particular employee might fall within, or if there are more significant issues affecting an employee, the only way to know more and get closer to a conclusion is to do what we do when we are trying to get to know someone—we ask questions. Only this time, you are *not* asking the employee, you are using your experience as a supervisor of this person to determine the proper way to engage, not categorize someone. Let me be perfectly clear, this is not about labeling individuals; this is about assessing the make up of your team and learning how to engage performers for greater productivity and career satisfaction. When a supervisor suspects that an employee's conduct attitude, or behavior is concerning, the supervisor can use the Scale to help balance the concerns; of course, always discuss the issues with someone in Human Resources. For you as a leader, these are observation and interaction questions to assess the employee's level of engagement. These questions are not to be used to interrogate employees. As stated above, you likely already have a sense of what an employee's tendencies are. These questions will help you make a better assessment of not where they fall, but of how to help.

> *"Employees worldwide who know their manager well "as a person" are more likely to be engaged."*
> Employee Engagement Report 2011
>
> *Beyond the Numbers: A Practical Approach for Individuals, Managers, and Executives*
> Published Dec 2010/Jan 2011

Once you have a sense of the at-risk employee's tendencies, you can then move into recovery mode. This is the point where you work to improve your engagement and his or her satisfaction. Consider these questions when considering the employee's performance and level of engagement:

Trapped Workers

- Are they inexperienced for the job they now hold?
- Do they miss deadlines or other important targets or goals?

- Do they lack key skills or qualifications?
- Is there a credibility issue because of a flaw in their conduct, attitude, and/or behavior?
- Are they unable to maneuver the corporate political environment?
- Do they lack political savvy?
- Do they lack sensitivity to others?
- Does there appear to be a disconnect between what is/is not appropriate?
- Do they lack the ability to be confidential?
- Do they read people poorly?
- Are they too candid?
- Do they exhibit poor interpersonal skills?

Entrepreneurs

- Do they get excited about doing new things or testing new concepts?
- Do they contribute a fair share of new or innovative ideas, or suggestions for improvements?
- Do their ideas seem so innovative that they may appear a little off base?
- Are they self-motivated?
- Are they always looking to learn more?
- Are they broadly experienced?
- Do they make political missteps?

- Are they widely viewed as overly ambitious?
- Can they generate new ideas, but they are unable to create related strategies?
- Are they unable to swing from strategic to tactica,l, and visa versa, when called to do so?

The Satisfied Performer

- Can they be counted on to deliver consistent results?
- Are they respected performers?
- Do they have a good understanding of the direction of the business?
- Are they customer focused?
- Do they know how to find solutions to challenges?
- Do their career goals align with business direction?
- Are they seen as team players?
- Are the employees is likeable?
- They are content in current roles, but could be considered for more visible or promotional opportunities if they are a good fit.
- They appear well-balanced personally and professionally.
- They accept challenges in their current role.
- Are often used to help bring onboard the new hires.
- Though not perfect, they do possess admirable conduct, attitudes, and behaviors.

The Checked-Out Performer

- Do they consistently resist change initiatives?
- Do they demonstrate passive-aggressive behaviors?
- Do they resist learning something new as it relates to their particular job?
- Are they comfortable operating in the status quo (so it may appear they are a Satisfied Performer)?
- Is their performance marginal at best?
- Do they rely too heavily on one set of skills or strengths for performance?
- Assess their level of engagement as it relates to contributing new ideas.
- Do they have difficulty with follow-through?
- Do they consistently miss deadlines?
- Are they, in general, disengaged, and seem as if their minds are elsewhere?

The Up-and-Comer

- Do they lack humility?
- Do they relish being the center of attention?
- Are they unable or unwilling to admit mistakes?
- Are they unclear on how to align their career with company goals?
- Are they not good listeners?

- Do they appear overly competitive?
- Are they unable to have successful collaborative work relationships?
- Do they have difficulty grasping strategic perspectives?
- Do they lack key skills or qualifications?
- Are they unable to maneuver the corporate political environment?
- Does there appear to be a disconnect between what is/is not appropriate?
- Do they read people poorly?
- Are they not seen as resourceful?
- Do they each rely too much on one particular strength?

Your take on these kinds of questions when engaging performers will help build a meaningful conversation and help you think through how you might best be suited to offer assistance, coaching, support, development, and guidance.

Addressing
Performance

"The conventional definition of management is getting work done through people, but real management is developing people through work."

—Agha Hasan Abedi

Addressing Performance

Addressing performance when performance is good is a piece of cake for anyone. You are happy, they are happy, and life is good. Now enter the performance issue, and no one is happy—mostly because having to tell someone they are not as good as you hoped, or as they might think they are, really stinks. There is no easy way of dealing with this leadership responsibility except to face it head on. Beyond being likeable, there are at least three major challenges that people managers have when it comes to performance improvement of a direct report: fear, interest, and listening. First we'll review the likable performer and then we'll take a look at the major challenges people managers face when it comes to performance improvement: fear, interest, and listening.

Likeability

Is the employee likeable? We know that firing someone because he or she is not likeable is weak, very weak, and not at all what we are suggesting. But we make hiring decisions routinely based on how well we connect with or "like" someone. The more we connect with a person, the more we tend to like a person. This is what great friendships, marriages, and work relationships are made of. Now enter the employee who is challenged and not at all likeable. Now what do you do?

There are great debates going on today about whether "likeability" is important or relevant to the work environment. If we were to view this completely objectively, we'd probably say "no," it is not relevant. As long as the work is getting done, I don't have to like you. But, what if, in order for the work to get done, you have to relate to me in a positive way? Now enter likeability. If I do not like you, and it's clear you do not like me, what is the likelihood we are going to relate well to one another? What then is the likelihood we are going to be productive? What if the dislike is related to age, race, ethnicity, gender, religion, or sexual orientation, for example?

This dislike can show up in words like, "we aren't connecting," or "I'm getting a funny vibe from her and don't want to work on this project with her," for example. Sometimes it shows up in passive-aggressive behavior that sabotages the success of a project or workstream.

This could be simply that you have an employee whose conduct, attitude, and behavior leave a lot to be desired. In these instances, encourage the employee to see someone in HR or to call the EAP to discuss challenges more fully. For others, you might need to encourage them to find a mentor (you might act in this role to help them understand the internal politics). Some might still need help through coaching with a certified professional coach, which is often reserved for those in higher pay grades. When you are unsure if it is related to the employee's conduct, attitude, or behavior, then thoughtful leaders can do the following:

- Assess if there are any patterns of behavior toward groups of people similar to the challenged employee within the organization that cause concern.

- Evaluate performance ratings for any hidden biases.

- Examine how training is awarded. Examine the makeup of those individuals for whom the company is making an investment. Are hidden- or early-potential employees being left out or over looked?

- Check to see if individuals have been complaining to human resources about issues within their department. Is anyone in HR seeing any patterns of behaviors that might be cause for concern?

- Are you seeing certain individuals excluded from group events, projects, or task forces? If so, explore why. Is it a matter of their conduct, attitude, and/or behavior, or is there something else going on?

Keep in mind that sometimes there are people that just do not get along. If the job assignment is important, and their job is tied to that assignment, sometimes you will have to force them to get over the issue for the good of the company without any further analysis. If they know that their performance is tied to one another, just maybe they will figure out a way to get the job done and exceed expectations regardless of their personal dislike of one another.

This type of analysis can give you a picture of the underlying currents, of which you might be unaware, that exist within the company, and allow you to address them early. A little trend analysis can go along way in engaging employees and exploring more fully if the issue is really the employee's conduct, attitude, and behavior, or if there are other challenges within the company. The affected employee believes that if they see something you see it too, but we know that this is not always the case. We must do our best to be more aware of, and address, challenges that will naturally arise when you get people together to accomplish a single goal.

Fear

There are at least three types of fear, listed below, that many people managers have a tough time addressing, especially when it has to do with an employee's conduct, attitude, and behavior:

- Fear of confrontation – the belief that something negative will occur during the discussion and the manager's uncertainty about how to respond.

- Fear of being sued – the fear that the manager, company, or both, might get named in a lawsuit that turns into a public-relations and financial nightmare. Related fear is that this could jeopardize the manager's job.

- Fear of violence – the ultimate fear has to be this one. The manager's fear is that the employee could do irreparable harm to themselves, the manager, coworkers, family, innocent bystanders, or customers.

You cannot change what you are not willing to confront. I have personally seen and been involved in highly volatile and violent employee issues. At the core of most of these situations was the manager's unwillingness to confront a bad attitude, poor performance, or behavior that did not line up to standards at the onset. There are no second chances when evaluating performance. If employees are not properly corrected by the manager the first time, they will repeat the same behaviors in the same way, if not worse. Many times, the manager does not know how to correct performance. HR's role must not be to hold the managers' hands, but to teach them the proper way to engage employees. Engaging employees does not come naturally for many people. I made it a habit to script leaders, coach them, and practicing with them, and then send them out. Immediately following the meeting, we would review what actually took place to see if there were any gaps that needed to be filled, or if I needed to provide any damage control.

These fears are very real and managers should not discount them in anyway. People managers need to be coached with each situation and sometimes pushed to confront poor performers. If managers are not held accountable for the performance of their staff, then perhaps leading people is not something they should be doing. If you approach every situation with a genuine sense of respect for the person with whom you are going to have an intense conversation, you will find yourself more at ease and able to choose words that are reflective of that inner peace.

Interest

There is a saying that "people don't care what you know until they know that you care." Showing genuine interest in the individual working for you can be the difference between an engaged performer and an actively disengaged performer. This results in a level of productivity that is either more or less satisfactory to your people managers.

So how does one take a genuine interest? First, care about the person—this is the key to being genuine. People know if you care or not about them. There is something in your eyes, your smile, your words, and your body language that sends a message about your true feelings. Figure out a way to convey genuine concern for your direct reports. Next, show you care by asking them about things important to them. First, you have to start with small talk. From there you learn little things that you will have to remember and, as often as possible, ask about the little things.

Listening

Although we have already adequately covered the art of listening in this instrument, it bears additional emphasis. Listening is closely connected to having genuine interest as discussed above, and is very critical indeed. This skill is about having respect for another person's thoughts, ideas, and opinions. The people who work for you have had experiences that could have a positive influence on decisions you make about your customers, your work, your products, and your services. There is safety in a multitude of counselors, so who is working on your team and has ideas or thoughts about the work, and to whom you should be listening? Have you asked and waited for input, ideas, and suggestions? Do you have a door that is open, or do you say it is open and in reality it is closed? In leadership, or one-on-one meetings, are you caught up in your daily or weekly monologue, or is there group discussion and dialogue taking place? Performers want and need to demonstrate value by offering their input. Even if you don't use them, take them in and seriously consider their suggestions. Finally, create time to just listen—call them listening sessions. Bring in some food and beverages, invite a group of performers, and just listen to whatever is on their minds. You will find it is powerful stuff.

There are, no doubt, a number of additional ways to begin engaging performers; however, people managers must learn to address, and move beyond, their own fears before they can tap into, and address, the concerns of their direct reports.

Change Management

"Ten years ago, Peter Senge introduced the idea of the 'learning organization.' Now he says that for big companies to change, we need to stop thinking like mechanics and to start acting like gardeners."

—*Alan M. Webber*

Change Management

However pressing the need for a change may be, it is rarely taken on a positive note by human beings. In organizations, when a large-scale change is about to be implemented, it often creates a high-stress environment in the organization. This condition happens because of an elevated level of stress and anxiety among the organization's employees. Most people face high stress levels due to change because they believe that they are not good enough to accomplish something that they have never accomplished before, and this leads to a feeling of denial, which is followed by disdain toward, or resistance to, the change.

To create a positive and sure-shot plan for implementation of a change in conduct, attitude, and behavior in an organization, it is important to minimize the risk that can act as a hindrance. Given below are some guidelines that you can use to minimize risk and support the transformation during a change:

Understand the goal and break it down into objectives

Making a radical break from past behaviors is difficult to accomplish, and leaders can expect to receive a great deal of resistance from employees because of its sudden nature and sheer magnitude. Instead of going for a long, intensive change, leaders can opt for a change that offers employees quick wins. Quick-win changes are beneficial because they allow smaller, achievable goals that are very easily accepted by the employees and, in a good coaching conversation, employees will come up with a few things they can change quickly. These quick wins, if done properly and constructively, lead to the accomplishment of long-term changes.

Preempt resistance to the change process

While formulating the necessary requirements and specific nuances of a change in conduct, attitude, and behavior is critical, make sure to include the employee's insight on how to design the transition process. Let the employee know what feedback will be given, reassure the employee that you will be supportive with training and development as needed, and remind the employee to tap in to the expertise of those in the Employee Assistance Program. However, make certain the employee knows that, while every opportunity will be given to make the change, failure to make sustained changes could result in separation. This added little bit of pressure indicates that the employee is ultimately responsible for making the adjustment.

Be flexible to accommodate differences

Many times, during the transition process, an employee may face challenges and offer alternative solutions for getting to the desired result. During the creation of a change initiative, it is necessary to include a provision for easy inclusion of different views and feedback throughout the process. Give yourself room to change your mind and make modifications along the way.

Explore the possibility of using external consultants to retrain employees

If you see that a transition is significant enough that an employee or group simply cannot make the change on their own, or the change requires a new or different skillset, provisions for the inclusion of external consultants and related coaching for employee training and development should be made. Instead of the entire workforce attempting to adopt a new set of skills, when practical, a limited number of employees should be trained at a time, and positive progress must be encouraged.

Document every action so that you can correct any mistakes made in the process

Last, but not the least, in an organization, no matter how much care is taken, mistakes can be made while working with employees to implement a change or transition. You must diligently prepare proper documentation of the change and its steps to prevent these mistakes.

Why Typical Engagement Strategies Won't Work for Everyone

Why Typical Engagement Strategies Won't Work for Everyone

No matter how much we try to ensure every employee feels respected, understood, recognized, and engaged, as leaders we must recognize that not everyone will buy in. Not everyone will offer their personal best—some because they won't, and others because they can't. With most performers, salary adjustments, listening, encouragement, training, development, improved peer and leader relationships, positive work environment, and teambuilding can lead to satisfactory and improved performance. However, others will need help beyond what you can give them in your leadership role.

After you have done everything you can to ensure your staff members know what is expected of them, and the systems for rewards and recognition are aligned, if an employee's conduct, attitude, and behavior fall below expectations and standards of performance, you have to move quickly to address the situation. To ignore an employee's behavior is equal to ignoring an open wound:

1. Is the employee is doing everything within the scope of the area of responsibility to meet or exceed expectations?
2. Is the employee qualified to perform the job, in other words, is the job fit appropriate for the skills, abilities, and interests of the employee?
3. Has the employee sought development in growth areas?
4. Is the company supporting the employee's need to maintain competence in the job and to perform at an optimal level?

If the job fit is appropriate for the employee's requisite skills and abilities, then it moves to a question of what is going on beyond basic knowledge, skills, and abilities. Either the employee wants to do the job and can't, or the employee can perform the job but isn't really interested.

Let's take a look at those who aren't buying in because they don't want to. There also those who, either passively or aggressively, refuse to get on board with the direction you are taking them or the direction of the company. If after speaking with them, listening, and exploring options, it is clear that they understand what is expected but won't step up to the plate and perform satisfactorily—perhaps it is time for them to move on. Unfortunately, some of these performers take calculated stands against leadership and culture shifts because they hold some type of influence in the company. They might have generated high sales, have built a strong customer following, or have hoarded knowledge and information to which no one else has access. When someone has the aptitude to perform, and are not willing to adhere to the culture and environment you are trying to build or rebuild, the risk of not dealing with their conduct, attitude, and behavior is that they have the potential to poison the entire team, and sometimes others, more broadly.

What can you do about those who just cannot seem to get it together? Initially, you might take it personally—that perhaps they are being defiant and/or just don't care. While those reasons might be true, it could be that something deeper is going on. Regardless of what you think about either scenario, you owe it to yourself, the employees, and the company to recognize when employees need help beyond what you can offer. If they don't respond to overtures of engagement over time, then perhaps they need help beyond what you can give. How do you recognize these people and what happens when you do?

Below is a limited list of warning signs that an employee might need to seek outside counsel:

1. Chronic complainers. No matter what you do, they are not satisfied and consistently sabotage the morale of the group.

2. Severely depressed. These individuals exhibit a decline in their ability to experience enjoyment or happiness and/or they are increasingly sad, or express a feeling of hopelessness.

3. Expresses thoughts of suicide or death—beyond the fear of dying. Perhaps they become fascinated with death and dying or they talk about death being a "better place" than where they are now.

4. Cannot let go of the past: Repeatedly brings up the good ole days, or appear emotionally tied to the past, so much that it prevents them from moving forward with new leadership, strategies, concepts, rules, and directions.

5. Appear unable to focus or concentrate on their goals or even conversations. If they consistently or repeatedly discuss unfavorable events, or unpleasant thoughts pop into their minds from which they don't seem to be able to escape, they may need outside counsel.

6. Increasingly impulsive. They exhibit unusual and extreme risky behaviors.

7. Increased irritability. Argumentative, sudden outbursts, or being easily annoyed.

8. Increasingly unable to get along with others. Has an unusual fixation of dislike for an employee or certain groups of employees.

While this list is not exhaustive, and there are many other related symptoms that accompany more severe behaviors, supervisors who are concerned should report the behavior to Human Resources who, together with the supervisor, can discuss the behaviors with employee and make appropriate recommendations. Never try approaching an employee directly about highly-sensitive behavioral challenges, this is best left up to trained professionals. If however, you find you need to take charge immediately, try the following strategies:

- Show genuine concern for the employee. If you do not believe you can, or if trying comes off as unbelievable to the employee, you will only make matters worse. In such cases, allow HR or a licensed professional handle the problem.

- With discharges, always work with an outplacement specialist to discuss the separation and the employee's feelings with a trained specialist immediately following the separation discussion—while the employee is still on site. Believe it or not, if an employee speaks immediately with a neutral third party about his or her rights and the next steps, the employee can be led to an emotional level that will allow focus, rational thought, and concentration on an immediate list of things to do, which will reduce the threat of any type of negative or retaliatory behaviors.

- Refer the employee to the Employee Assistance Program when appropriate. EAP programs are fantastic, underutilized services to the company that can help address and even resolve less severe situations.

- If you ever feel you or your team is in danger, act quickly and rationally. Do not try to be a superhero. Avoid embarrassing the employee or bringing unwanted attention to them publicly. If the employee is loud, boisterous, or belligerent, respond in a calm voice, make eye contact, preserve their dignity, and get them and anyone around to a place of calm and safety until authorities arrive on the scene.

Clearly, in some of these are more extreme cases, however, we must recognize that some people need help beyond our skills as supervisor. When you recognize that some people need professional help, it makes your job as a leader much easier knowing that there is help for them beyond the walls of the office. You have resources in your HR department, EAP program, outplacement specialists, and the police, if needed. Your job is to ensure there is minimal interruption to the workflow and the environment, and that the safety of employees is preserved.

A final word of caution—recognize when diversity issues are in play and address them immediately. In some companies, diversity issues run deep. Some companies have obvious issues, whereas other companies are more discrete. Regardless, leaders must be open to the idea that the employee's performance could be severely and negatively impacted. When domestic violence and severely negative personal issues are impact performance, make certain not to play counselor, but refer the employee to HR who can connect them with the EAP, local authorities, and crisis centers for attention. Consultation with HR is critical when addressing performance issues with employees for these reasons.

The Engagement
Process

"You do not lead by hitting people over the head — that's assault, not leadership."

— Dwight D. Eisenhower

The Engagement Process

Now that we have addressed performance issues, mitigating risk to change, and how to recognize employees who need more significant help, let's take a look at each of the five performance types and explore how a supervisor can now begin the engagement process with performers who do not have severe extenuating circumstances.

The Trapped Worker	The Entrepreneur
It is going to take some time to pull them into the Satisfied Performer's club because there may be an issue of trust. Build their trust, follow-through on your word, and reward their efforts.	These individuals need structure and assimilation into the company culture. You'll have to coach them and work with them on being patient. Teach them the value of working through people and systems.
The Satisfied Performer	
Word of caution, do not forsake these performers and leave them to their own devices. Though happy, they will not be ignored and could easily fall into one of the other four quadrants, easily. Keep them engaged, informed and rewarded. Don't leave them out of the loop and continue to show respect for their consistent performance.	
The Checked Out	The Up and Comer (Early and High Potentials)
These performers are going to be the toughest to transition into the Satisfied Performer's club because they may already think they are there. They are either happy about working towards retirement or happy about the prospect that they can wait the change out. Here you'll have to remind them the risk of driving a status quo CAB and follow-thru on your word.	These individuals need mentors, coaches and sponsors. Pair them with a senior person to mentor them, and a professional coach to help them take smarter strategic actions and make better decisions. When ready, find an internal person to sponsor them. As a leader, you'll have to forego the good ole boy way of climbing the corporate ladder and paying your dues mentality to truly engage these individuals. You'll only have them for 3-5 years, 7 if you're good, so get the most out of them before they go.

Keep in mind that we want to demonstrate genuine respect for performers, and believe that deep down inside they want to achieve results:

1. Recognize they have something to offer. Discuss this with them, pull out what they believe are their strengths. Explore if you are leveraging their strengths. Discuss and agree upon what you both believe are areas for opportunity, for growth, and for development. Ask them to design their career path in the company for the next 3-5 years. What does it look like? What are the steps to getting there? What does career satisfaction look and feel like?

2. Ask the employee what they believe is truly holding them back. Listen to them. Take note, acknowledge their concerns, make a commitment in the moment, and then take action. Do not forget to discuss and emphasize the importance of the work they are performing—they may have forgotten!

3. Ask them to research any suggestions or ideas that are presented in the meeting. Give them instruction on how to present a well-rehearsed, researched, fully-formed concept for you to consider.

4. Recognize that the employee may need support and supporters. If there have been political missteps, work with the employee on course correction. Invest your time building relationships with people who are guided by integrity and can discern between right and wrong. Commit to reskill and increase skills for performers with hidden and early potential. If you do this, it will create an expanded pool of talent without the additional expense the recruiting process takes.

5. Ask if they are taking care of themselves from a health and wellness perspective. Take care of your health and wellness. If you do not feel good, you will not look good or perform well. If you do not look good, you will not have the confidence to put your best foot forward.

6. Ask if they are taking advantage of the financial benefits the company is offering (retirement, 401K, 403B, etc.). Remind them that these are great benefits and will help them be prepared for a secure future.

7. Perhaps some have gone astray by being too outspoken or not speaking enough. Where does this person fall on the scale? Discuss this problem with them. Suggest ways for them to manage self-control. Tell the employee to speak up and do not give up! If they believe in their idea, tell them to get used to the word "no," but get over it quickly, listen to the "why," retool and go back. If they do not succeed, tell them to save it for another time.

8. Are you a finger-pointing leader? Do you ask "who did that?" or "who's responsible?" before you understand the condition of the situation? Perhaps employees will be more honest and admit to mistakes, or even take risks if they were given the room to fail, because, as Victor Kiam states, "even if you fall on your face, you are still moving forward."

9. Be forward thinking. Ask them what they truly think about the future of the company. Ask them, "What are we missing?"

10. Be honest, direct, and caring. If the employee is not likeable, they need to know that fact—and the implications in the workplace. Some very smart people, who are fully capable, simply will not move forward because their conduct, attitude, and behavior is undesirable. Do not send a message on this one, that they will not understand unless it is delivered with credibility, trust, and caring. If you cannot deliver that message in this way, then leave it up to the professionals in HR to help.

11. Ensure that those workers who truly do want to retire from the company are executing an effective knowledge transfer plan. Understanding the nuances of a particular job or paying attention to details that a long-term worker might take for granted simply because of the routine, could easily trip up the person that follows. This plan should be in place at least one year before retirement. The message is clear, if employees are not engaged, the company suffers and knowledge is lost—not managed and retained. Having a preretirement program in place will make the transition, for both the retiring performer and the company, a very rewarding experience.

Bottom Line: Hand Them the Keys

"Progress always involves risk; you can't steal second base and keep your foot on first."

—— Frederick Wilcox

Bottom Line: Hand Them the Keys

When employees have input in the following six areas of performance, the company reaps significant benefits:

The Key: Who they work with

Company Benefit: They stay longer

Leading Company: **Valve Corp.**

Valve Corp. is a videogame maker in Bellevue, Washington. Valve, whose website says the company has been "boss free" since its founding in 1996, and has no managers or assigned projects. Instead, its three hundred employees recruit colleagues to work on projects they think are worthwhile. The company prizes mobility so much that workers' desks are mounted on wheels, allowing them to scoot around to form work areas as they choose. Welcome to the bossless company, where the hierarchy is flat, pay is often determined by peers, and the workday is directed by the employees themselves. Source: online.wsj.com

The Key: What they are working on

Company Benefit: Productivity increases. You get more customers, and revenue goes up!

Leading Company: **DreamWorks**

At DreamWorks, employees are allowed to pitch a movie concept, all workers are given access to artist development courses, and they are allowed to take risks and learn from mistakes instead of being fired. "We challenge all our employees to be their own CEOs," says Dan Satterthwaite, head of human resources. Source: USAToday.com

The Key:	When the work gets done
Company Benefit:	Absenteeism decreases, their time and attendance improves
Leading Company:	**PNC Financial Services Group, Inc.**

"Nearly half of our 25,000 employee work force is on some type of flexible arrangement, including job sharing, telecommuting, and compressed work weeks," says Darcel Kimble of PNC's corporate communications group. A 2005 study by the non-profit organization Corporate Voices for Working Families found that a compressed work week pilot program at PNC resulted in: work that had previously taken two days being done in one day; absenteeism dropping from 60 days to nine days; improved customer service; and the company saving over $100,000 in turnover costs. Source: Careerbuilder.com

The Key:	Where the work gets done
Company Benefit:	The employee becomes your word of mouth advocate.
Leading Company:	**Meddius**

Jeff Gunther, CEO of the Charlottesville, VA-based software company Meddius, decided he would change the way his staff works by instituting a results-only working environment, often referred to as a

ROWE. Meddius employees can work any time from any place in any way, as long as they get their work done. Gunther has found that by giving employees the trust and autonomy they need, they have actually been more productive and loyal to the company. Source: Inc.com

The Key:	Why the work is important
Company Benefit:	Employees give you their best ideas
Leading Company:	**Danone UK Ltd.**

Group Danone is the world leader in fresh dairy products and second in bottled water and baby foods. It employs nearly 90,000 people in more than 80 countries. Danone UK Ltd is in the dairy business. Products include Actimel, and Activia. The company spends time educating employees through stories about the difference Activia can make, and associated medical conditions. There is a clear belief with the organization that purpose is crucial and drives employee engagement. In 2009 Danone UK Ltd won the Number 1 Great Place to Work Award. Source: www.cipd.co.uk

The Key:	How the work gets done
Company Benefit:	Job satisfaction increases
Leading Company:	**Microsoft**

Microsoft employees in Redmond, Washington are not only given the opportunity to decide how their work gets done, but, in September 2012, Microsoft continued a tradition of equipping employees with the tools to do so, including Windows Phone 8 and Surface tablets for use at work or at home. Source:www.geekwire.com

Identify what will work for your company or organization. You should pilot and test new ideas before broad implementation whenever possible. Remain flexible and open to try different strategies for different work group configurations. The double bottom line: take care of employees and they will take care of you.

Measuring Success

Measuring Success

We all want to be successful in whatever we endeavor. Working with and leading people requires that, as leaders, we take extra steps and make extra efforts to ensure their success and our own. Every now and then, we should stop and ask ourselves "is it working?" Are the strategies we've employed, the styles we've adopted, the structures we've put in placed really bringing us the success we desire? Below are the additional questions people managers should ask themselves as they assess their leadership:

1. How do you know that your coaching is working?

2. How do you measure if a leader is actually putting time and effort into ensuring the talent is engaged?

3. How can you report on the progress of this or any engagement program?

4. How do you minimize risk to the organization?

5. How do you turn this into dollars and cents?

Consider the following steps if you truly seek to improve the pace of employee engagement in your organization:

1. Measure the year to year increase or decrease in the number of referrals that come from staff. If your staff is not encouraging external candidates to work for your company, what is the message?

2. Establish a guideline for the percent of hires that should be internal. Measure the number of individuals who apply for internal promotional opportunities.

3. Track innovation. How much revenue is the company generating from new ideas?

4. Track the employee engagement-survey statistics. Measure what is important to *them,* not just what is important to the company leaders.

5. Measure client satisfaction and growth in new business, not just retained or repeat business.

6. Measure leaders by the number of leaders they are developing and grooming for next-level opportunities.

7. Bring back the 360 degree assessment.

8. Evaluate the increase or decrease in stress-related health claims.

9. Track employee complaints, EEOC charges filed, and other related activities that point to an unhappy worker or workforce. Are these numbers increasing or decreasing?

10. Break down engagement surveys into the satisfaction of diverse workers. Are there any red flags in a particular area?

11. Evaluate how diverse workers feel about the work environment, if their needs are being adequately met, and if they are being given training and development opportunities at the same rate as their counterparts?

12. Measure and calculate the net change in productivity, training, turnover, sales, time spent in meetings, absenteeism, tardiness, efficiency, and worker's compensation.

13. Are you seeing a decreased need to use consultants and outside contractors? This is a sign that more work is being generated internally without the repeated need for external consultation on a widespread scale.

Hold leaders accountable for the engagement and satisfaction of all their employees, not just the high performers. Remember, this is not a wholesale process, analyzing the entire company all at one time. This is to be used one leader, and one department or business unit at a time. Trying to transform an entire culture all at once is like trying to boil the ocean. Start where engagement is needed most and go from there. In a very short time, you will see the attitude of the workforce transform.

Bibliography

Amabile, Teresa, and Steven Kramer. "Do Happier People Work Harder?" Editorial. N.p., 3 Sept. 2011. Web.

Bishop, Todd. "Microsoft Employees Getting Free Surface Tablets, New Work PCs, Windows Phone 8." GeekWire. N.p., 13 Sept. 2012. Web. 28 Dec. 2012.

Blessing White. *Beyond the Numbers: A Practical Approach for Individuals, Managers and Executives.* Rep. N.p.: Blessing White, 2011. Print.

Bruzzese, Anita. "USA TODAY." USATODAY.COM. USA Today, 23 July 2012. Web. 28 Dec. 2012.

Lapowsky, Issie. "10 Things Employees Want Most." Inc.com. N.p., 27 Aug. 2010. Web. 28 Dec. 2012.

"5 Flextime-Friendly Companies." 5 Flextime-Friendly Companies. Career Builder, 18 Dec. 2009. Web. 28 Dec. 2012.

"10 Minutes on Engaging Your Pivotal Talent." Issue brief. N.p.: PricewaterhouseCoopers, LLC, 2010. Print.

Power Project Institute, LLC Research Report. "Viability of the Human Resource Operation in the Market." 2012–2013

"Shared Purpose and Sustainable Organisation Performance." Rep. London: CIPD, 2009. Print.

Silverman, Rachel E. "Who's the Boss? There Isn't One." WSJ.com. Wall Street Journal, 19 June 2012. Web. 28 Dec. 2012.

"The Post-Recession Workplace." Alexandria: Society for Human Resource Management, 2010. Print.

World Health Organization. Protecting Worker's Health Series. Rep. no. 3. Nottingham UK: World Health Organization, 2005. Print.

About Power
Project Institute, LLC

OUR MISSION

We provide our clients with innovative employee engagement strategies and effective career development programs that help them become more resourceful, responsible, and capable of achieving their desired results.

OUR VISION

The Power Project Institute is an employee engagement and career development organization established to provide innovative and cost-effective solutions that address the common challenges facing companies and independent professionals today.

We build resourceful companies—

We believe in the power of leveraging untapped, underutilized, and overlooked talent to transform organizations. We provide sustainable strategies that help our clients improve their performance, while maximizing employee attraction, engagement, satisfaction, and retention.

We build resourceful leaders—

are the "resourceful leadership" experts. We provide innovative training and development programs that empower leaders to take responsibility for their results and embrace challenges as opportunities.

We build resourceful careers—

We believe professionals should succeed at the level they deserve. We provide dynamic programs that help individuals take control of their careers so they can get the respect, recognition, and results they want at work.

OUR CORE VALUES

Exceed expectations—

We will consistently deliver our best performance, attitude, and service because we exceed our employee's expectations.

Inspire excellence—

Innovation and creativity comes from people. Every person has something to offer. Our goal is not to pull it out but to cause it to spring forth!

Enjoy life—

If life is either a daring adventure or nothing at all, we will responsibly encourage the former at every engagement, interaction, and opportunity.

Made in the USA
Lexington, KY
07 January 2015